FARM MACHINES

COMBINE

KATHY MIDDLETON

A Crabtree Roots Book

Crabtree Publishing
crabtreebooks.com

School-to-Home Support for Caregivers and Teachers

This book helps children grow by letting them practice reading. Here are a few guiding questions to help readers build comprehension skills. Possible answers appear here in red.

Before Reading:

- What do I think this book is about?
    - *I think this book is about combines.*
    - *I think this book will talk about what combines do.*
- What do I want to learn about this topic?
    - *I want to learn about what jobs combines do.*
    - *I want to learn why combines are important farm machines.*

During Reading:

- I wonder why...
    - *I wonder why farmers use a combine.*
    - *I wonder why combines are needed on a farm.*
- What have I learned so far?
    - *I have learned that combines have a reel.*
    - *I have learned that combines have a cutter bar.*

After Reading:

- What details did I learn about this topic?
    - *I have learned that some combines separate grain from other parts of the plant.*
    - *I learned that combines do work when crops are finished growing.*
- Read the book again and look for the vocabulary words.
    - *I see the word **combine** on page 3 and the word **crops** on page 4. The other vocabulary words are found on page 14.*

This is a **combine**.

Combines cut **crops** on a farm.

A **reel** lifts plants up to be cut.

A **cutter bar** cuts the plants.

Combines separate the **grain** from other parts of the plant.

The rest of the plant goes out the back of the combine.

Word List

Sight Words

a
after
and
are
be
cut
do
from
growing
is
lifts
of
on
other
parts
plants
separate
the
this
to

Words to Know

combine

crops

cutter bar

grain

reel

46 Words

This is a **combine**.

Combines cut **crops** on a farm.

A **reel** lifts plants up to be cut.

A **cutter bar** cuts the plants.

Combines separate the **grain** from other parts of the plant.

The rest of the plant goes out the back of the combine.

COMBINE

Written by: Kathy Middleton
Designed by: Under the Oaks Media
Proofreader: Crystal Sikkens
Production manager: Candice Campbell
Prepress technician: Katherine Kantor

Photographs: All images from Sutterstock

Crabtree Publishing

crabtreebooks.com 800-387-7650

 In Canada: We acknowledge the financial support of the Government of Canada through the Canada Book Fund for our publishing activities.

Printed in the U.S.A./CP2025

Published in Canada
Crabtree Publishing
616 Welland Ave.
St. Catharines, Ontario
L2M 5V6

Published in the United States
Crabtree Publishing
347 Fifth Ave
Suite 1402-145
New York, NY 10016

Library and Archives Canada Cataloguing in Publication
Available at Library and Archives Canada

Library of Congress Cataloging-in-Publication Data
Available at the Library of Congress

Hardcover: 978-1-0398-8106-8
Paperback: 978-1-0398-8467-0
Ebook (pdf): 978-1-0398-8226-3
Epub: 978-1-0398-8346-8
Audio: 978-1-0398-8509-7
Read-Along: 978-1-0398-8551-6